Collins

easy … g

First Time French

workbook

Ages 5–7

Je m'appelle
[My name is]

....

How to use this book

- Look at the left-hand page first to familiarize yourself with the vocabulary being covered.
- Use the pronunciation given for each word to help you to pronounce words correctly.
- Read out the instructions clearly and ensure children understand what they have to do.
- Discuss with the children what they have learnt.
- Recap regularly and return to previous topics that the children have enjoyed.
- Reward children with plenty of praise and encouragement.
- Encourage children to say new words out loud. This will help them to practise speaking French, and help them to remember new words.
- Make learning French fun for you and your children!

Special features

- Yellow boxes: introduce and outline the key vocabulary and structures in French.
- Orange boxes: offer suggestions for other activities for children to consolidate their learning in different contexts.
- Orange shaded boxes: provide additional information about French language and culture.
- Blue boxes: give instructions for an activity to reinforce learning.

HarperCollins Publishers
Westerhill Road
Bishopbriggs
Glasgow
G64 2QT

HarperCollins Publishers
1st Floor, Watermarque Building,
Ringsend Road, Dublin 4, Ireland

HarperCollins Canada Ltd.
22 Adelaide Street W, 41st Floor Toronto,
ON, M5H 4E3

First Edition for Canada 2021
10 9 8 7 6 5 4 3 2 1

ISBN 978-0-00-847594-9

previously published as 978-0-00-815946-7

www.collins.co.uk

Printed and bound in
Great Britain by Martins The Printers

A catalogue record for this book is available from the British Library.

FOR THE PUBLISHER
Maree Airlie
Michelle l'Anson
Sarah Woods

ILLUSTRATIONS
Q2AMedia
Shutterstock

MAPS
© Collins Bartholomew Ltd

COVER IMAGE
Shutterstock
© James Weston

MIX
Paper from
responsible sources
FSC www.fsc.org FSC™ C007454

This book is produced from independently certified FSC™ paper to ensure responsible forest management.

For more information visit: www.harpercollins.co.uk/green

Contents

L'alphabet en français
The French alphabet

The French alphabet has the same number of letters as in English, but some of the letters are pronounced slightly differently.

A [ah]
B [bay]
C [say]
D [day]
E [euh]
F [eff]
G [zhay]
H [ash]
I [ee]
J [zhee]
K [kah]
L [ell]
M [em]
N [en]
O [oh]
P [pay]
Q [coo]
R [err]
S [ess]
T [tay]
U [oo]
V [vay]
W [doob-leh-vay]
X [eeks]
Y [eegrek]
Z [zed]

Try singing the French alphabet to the same tune as the English one or even to "Auld Lang Syne". You could play "Hangman", called **Le pendu** in French, using children's names or movie characters, saying the letters in French.

Did you know? French and English are both official languages of Canada, but in the province of Quebec, French is the only official language. French is also one of the national languages in many other countries, for example, France, Belgium, Switzerland and many parts of Africa, including Madagascar!

Connect the letters of the alphabet in order to draw a famous Canadian landmark. Once you have completed the picture, say the whole alphabet out loud in French.

Write out your name in fancy letters – bubble writing, different coloured pens, dot to dot – and practise saying each letter in French as you do it.

Bonjour!
Hello!

When you first start speaking French you want to be able to say the simple things. These two children are using French to greet each other.

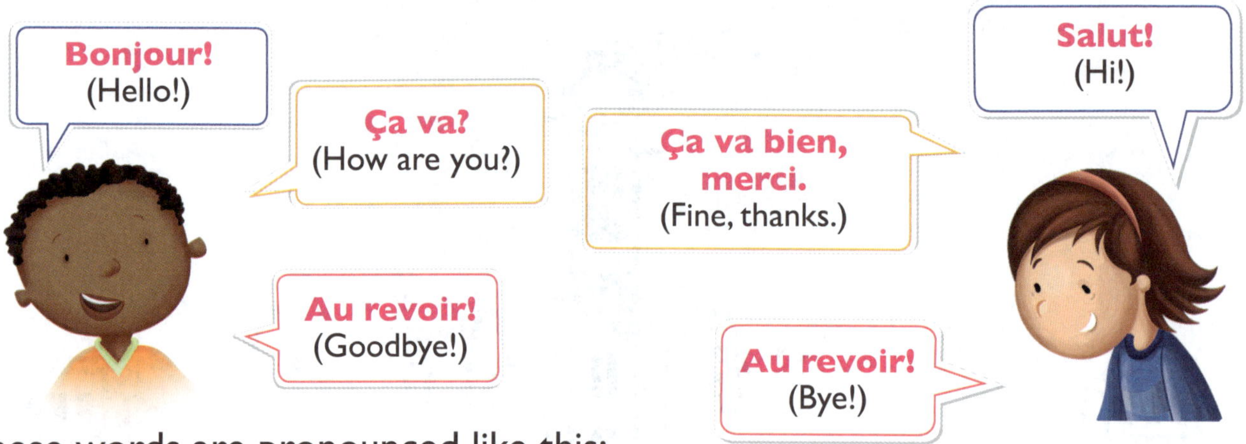

These words are pronounced like this:

bonjour [bongjoor]

au revoir [oh ruhvwar]

bien [beeyan]

salut [saloo]

ça va [sa va]

merci [mercee]

Other things you might like to say are:

oui [wee] meaning **yes** and **non** [nong] meaning **no**

s'il te plaît [seel tuh pleh] meaning **please**

de rien [duh reeyan] meaning **you're welcome**

comme çi, comme ça [comm see, comm sa] meaning **not too bad**

Use your fingers or make sock puppets to act out a short conversation, practising saying **bonjour** and **au revoir** and asking how someone is doing. Why not give your puppets a name and use them throughout this book to practise speaking French?

Did you know? In Quebec, people often give a kiss on the cheek when greeting each other. This greeting is known as **la bise**.

Look carefully at the French words given below and circle the one that is the odd one out. Can you also pronounce these words in French and say what they mean in English?

non	**oui**	**non**	**non**	**non**
salut	**salut**	**salut**	**salut**	**au revoir**
merci	**merci**	**salut**	**merci**	**merci**
oui	**oui**	**oui**	**non**	**oui**

Use pencil crayons to go over the dots to write out this French word. What does it say?

Bonjour

Now draw your own French dotty word.

Tout sur moi
All about me

One of the things you will want to do in French is to introduce yourself:

Je m'appelle...
[juh mappell]
My name is...

If you want to ask someone's name you can say:

Comment tu t'appelles?
[kommon too tappell]
What is your name?

Play this game with a partner: make a list of characters like the ones shown below. Choose a character for your partner to be. That person then has to guess which character you have chosen for them by asking **Je m'appelle...?** **Is my name...?** If they get it right, say **oui**, if they don't, say **non**, and they can try again. Make sure you both get a turn. Why not think of other characters, for example, cartoon characters, to play this game?

Ziggy

Bella

Nellie

Igor

Frosty

Did you know? Lots of names in English have a different form in French, for example, Andrew in French is André, Michael is Michel, and Peter is Pierre. Lots of girls' names in English already come from French, for example, Charlotte, Claire and Isabelle.

Draw a picture of yourself in the picture frame below. In the box write **bonjour** or **salut** and fill in your name.

____ !

Je m'appelle ______________________________________ .

Je sais compter (1-10)
I can count (1-10)

Here are the numbers you need to count up to ten in French:

1	2	3	4	5
un [ung]	**deux** [duh]	**trois** [trwa]	**quatre** [katr]	**cinq** [sank]
6	7	8	9	10
six [seess]	**sept** [set]	**huit** [weet]	**neuf** [nuhf]	**dix** [deess]

Other things you might like to say are:

plus [ploos] meaning **add (+)**

moins [mwang] meaning **minus (-)**

égale [aygal] meaning **equals (=)**

Try doing some sums in French:

deux plus trois égale cinq (2 + 3 = 5)

dix moins un égale neuf (10 - 1 = 9)

Practise counting in French in different ways – loudly and quietly, singing the numbers, even backwards from ten. Ask a partner to hold out their fingers and close their eyes. Number the fingers from 1 to 10, then touch any finger and ask them to say what number it is in French.

Look at these pictures and count the objects in French out loud.
Write the correct number under each picture.

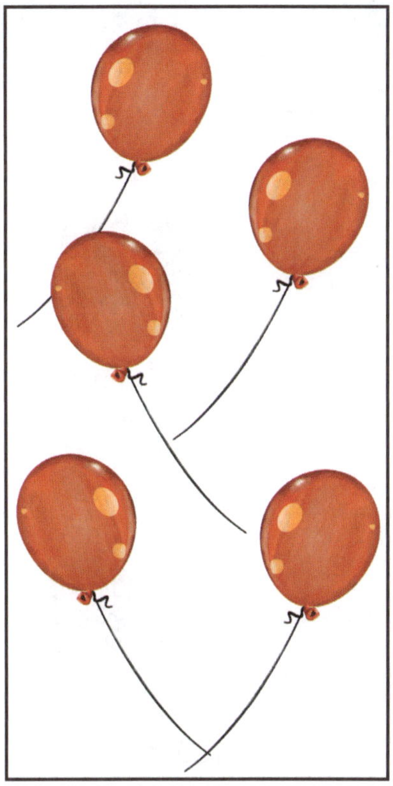

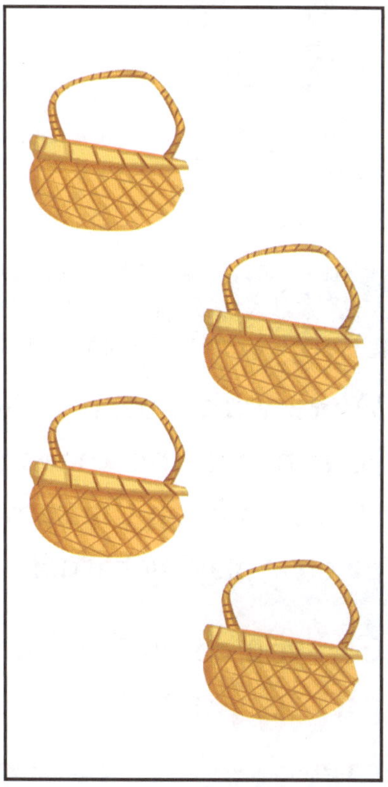

Je sais compter (11-20)
I can count (11-20)

Here are the numbers you need to count up to twenty in French:

11
onze
[onz]

12
douze
[dooz]

13
treize
[trez]

14
quatorze
[katorz]

15
quinze
[kanz]

16
seize
[sez]

17
dix-sept
[deess-set]

18
dix-huit
[deess-weet]

19
dix-neuf
[deess-nuhf]

20
vingt
[vang]

Work with a partner and count together or alternately up to 20, clapping your hands and knees while you are doing it. Speed up and slow down, trying to keep the same rhythm. Why not try some simple sums, using dice or playing cards?

Can you count from 0 to 20 backwards, or count up in twos?
deux, quatre, six...

Jeu : Lotto

Let's play **lotto**! Choose 5 numbers between 1 and 10 or 1 and 20 and write them down. Listen for your numbers to be called out in French – if you have written the number down on the sheet, you can cross it out. If you manage to cross out all the numbers, shout **'lotto'**!

Jeu 1

Jeu 2

Jeu 3

Les couleurs
Colours

These are the names of some of the colours in French:

bleu
[bluh]

rouge
[rooj]

vert
[vair]

jaune
[zhohn]

blanc
[blong]

noir
[nwar]

rose
[rose]

mauve
[mov]

orange
[oronge]

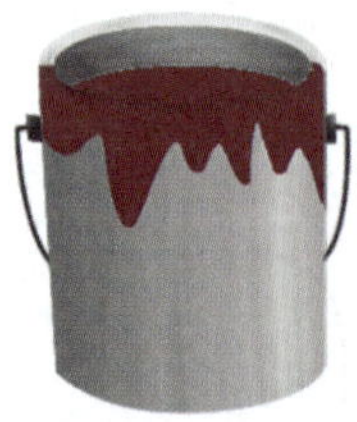

brun
[brung]

If you want to ask what colour something is, ask: **C'est de quelle couleur?** [se duh kell coolur]. The answer would be: **C'est…** [se] **It is…**

Play a version of "I spy" in French using colours instead of letters: **Je vois quelque chose de…** [zhe vwa kelka shows duh] **I can see something…** Guesses can be given in English or the object can be pointed at or held up.

Did you know? The national colours of Canada are red and white, as you can see on the Canadian flag.

The Quebecois flag is different from the Canadian flag, and is called **le fleurdelisé**. Colour it in using the colours shown.

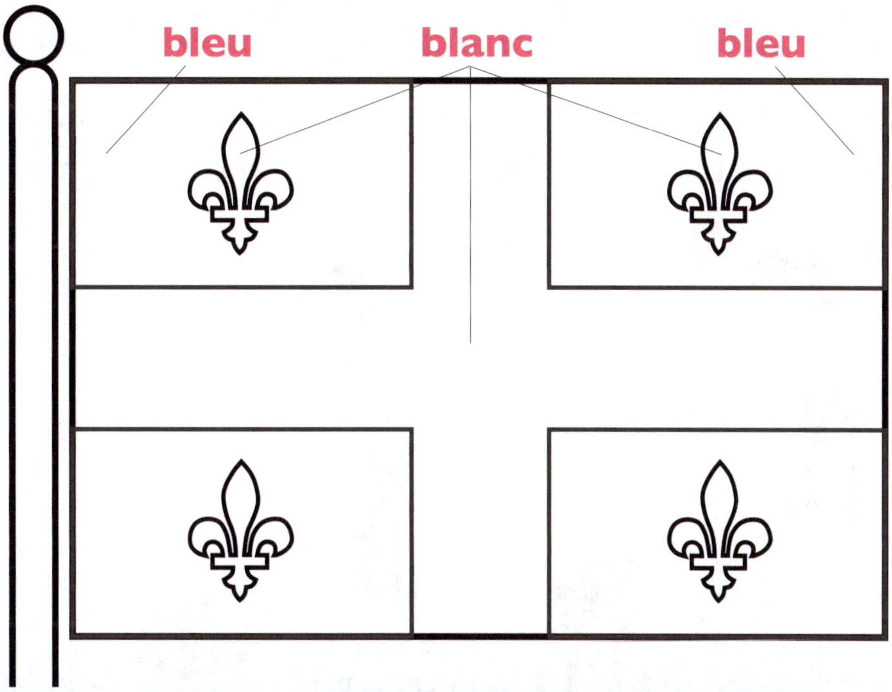

Colour in the **arc-en-ciel** [ark ong seeyell] using the colours given in French. There is a key under the picture to help you get the colours right.

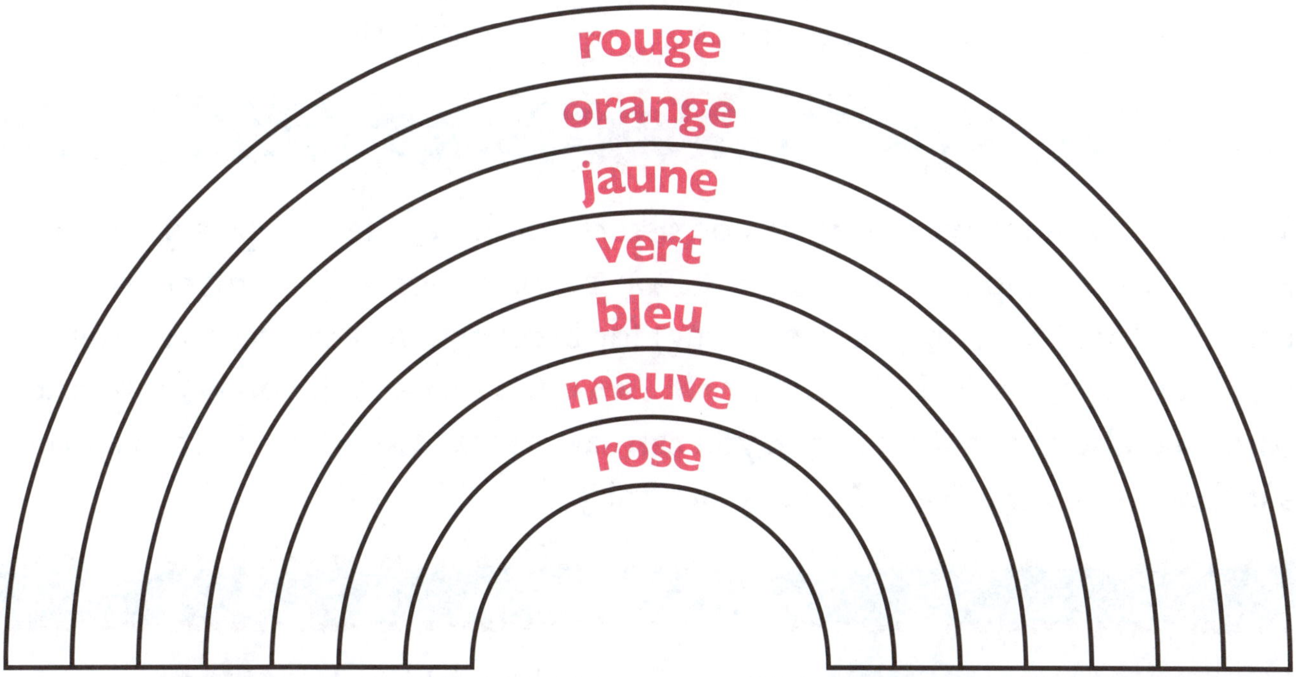

Ma famille
My family

To introduce members of your family, say: **Voici...** [vwasee] which means **Here is...** Remember to use **ma** [ma] for women and **mon** [mong] for men.

Voici...

...ma **maman**
[ma mamong]

...ma **sœur**
[ma suhr]

...ma **grand-mère**
[ma grong-mair]

...mon **papa**
[mong papa]

...mon **frère**
[mong frair]

...mon **grand-père**
[mong grong-pair]

To talk about how many brothers or sisters you have, use **J'ai** [zhay] meaning **I have**, for example: **J'ai une sœur** or **J'ai un frère**. Remember to use **une** [oon] for sisters and **un** [ung] for brothers. You can combine the sentences using **et** [ay]: **J'ai deux sœurs et un frère**. If you want to ask someone else about their family, you can say: **Tu as une sœur?** [too a oon suhr] or **Tu as un frère?** [too a ung frair].

Make a card for someone in your family, maybe wishing them **Happy Birthday** (**bonne fête**) or **Merry Christmas** (**joyeux Noël**) or saying **Congratulations!** (**Félicitations!**). Inside the card you could write **à** meaning **to** and **de** meaning **from**.

Draw your family (and friends) in the spaces below. For each person write their name after **voici**. Can you talk about your picture collage in French?

Voici__________

Voici__________

Voici__________

Voici__________

Voici__________

Les animaux
Pets

For many people, pets are just as important as other family members. To talk about your pets you can use **J'ai** as you did when talking about your family.

un **chien**
[ung sheeang]

un **poisson rouge**
[ung pwasong rooj]

un **lapin**
[ung lapang]

un **hamster**
[ung amstair]

un **chat**
[ung sha]

un **cochon d'Inde**
[ung koshon dand]

une **tortue**
[oon tortoo]

un **cheval**
[ung shuhval]

If you want to ask whether someone has a pet, you can say: **Tu as un animal?** [too ah ung anemaal]. The answer could be either **Oui, j'ai...** or **Non**. Remember to use **une** [oon] or **un** [ung] for the different pets. You can combine the sentences using **et** [ay]: **J'ai deux chats et un hamster**.

Work with a partner – one person acts out an animal, the other tries to guess what that animal is in French: **C'est un/une...?** [sett ung/oon] **Is it a...?** The answer would then be **oui** or **non**. You could learn a few more exotic animals to make it more fun, for example, **un serpent** [ung serpong] - a **snake**, or even **une tarentule** [oon tarentool] – a **tarantula**! To make your acting more authentic, why don't you make masks of the animals that you can wear?

Did you know? Roosters in French say **cocorico** [kohkohreekoh] and birds sing **cui cui** [kwee kwee]!

Jeu : Mots cachés

Can you find these six French pets in the square?

cheval **poisson** **chat** **chien** **lapin** **tortue**

p	c	h	i	e	n	c
o	c	h	a	t	i	u
i	l	a	p	i	p	x
s	c	h	e	v	a	l
s	q	n	w	h	l	r
o	e	u	t	r	o	t
n	x	u	b	e	b	s

Why not make up your own **Mots cachés** using some French words for pets?

____

____

____

____

____

____

Mon corps
My body

If you want to talk about different parts of the body in French, here are the most common words you might need.

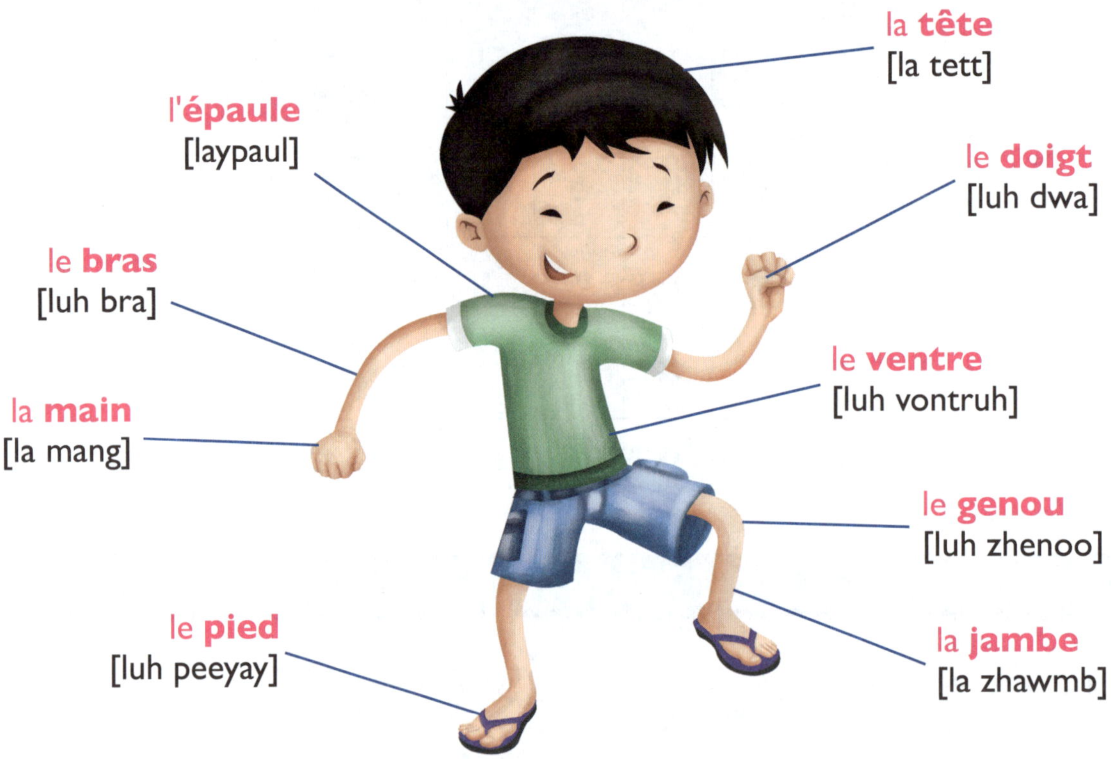

In order to practise these words, it might be helpful to learn the instruction **touchez...** [tooshay] – **touch...**!

Take a large piece of paper and draw the outline of a body on it, or even draw round someone lying on a very large piece of paper. Write the words for different parts of the body on sticky notes, then stick them on to the body in the correct place. You could put them on incorrectly and see if anyone spots which parts are wrong!

Did you know? There are two words for **toe** in French: **l'orteil** [lortay] and **le doigt de pied** [luh dwa duh peeyay]. The second one actually means "the finger of the foot".

Jeu : Beetle Drive

A good way to practise the words for parts of the body is to play a game of "Beetle Drive". The aim of the game is to draw a full person by rolling the appropriate numbers on the dice – each number represents a part of the body. Use the boxes below to draw in.

You need to roll a 6 first to start the game and draw **le torse** (the body). Then add on the other body parts as you roll them on the dice. The first player to complete their person shouts out **'Fini!'** [feenee] meaning **finished!** **Bonne chance!** – **Good luck!**

Numbers for each part of the body

1 = la **tête** 2 = la **jambe** 3 = le **bras** 4 = le **pied**
5 = la **main** 6 = le **torse**

Jeu 1

Jeu 2

Jeu 3

Jeu 4

Mon visage
My face

To talk about specific parts of your face in French, use the following vocabulary.

The French equivalent to the game "Simon says" is called **Jean dit** and is played in the same way. Instructions could be: **touchez...** [tooshay] – **touch...** or **secouez...** [seckooay] – **shake...** Of course, it is always fun to sing "Heads, shoulders, knees and toes" in French: **la tête, l'épaule, le genou, le pied ... les yeux, les oreilles, la bouche, le nez**.

Did you know? The word **dandelion** comes from the French **dent de lion** which means "lion's tooth". Apparently people thought that the leaves looked like the teeth of a lion.

Draw a monster's head, using your imagination to make it look as strange as you can! Write down the number of eyes, ears and so on that you have given your monster and show what colours you have used in the box below.

	Nombre	**Couleur**
bouche		
yeux		
oreilles		
dents		
nez		

Mon étui à crayons
My pencil case

Here are the French words for some of the items that might be found in a pencil case:

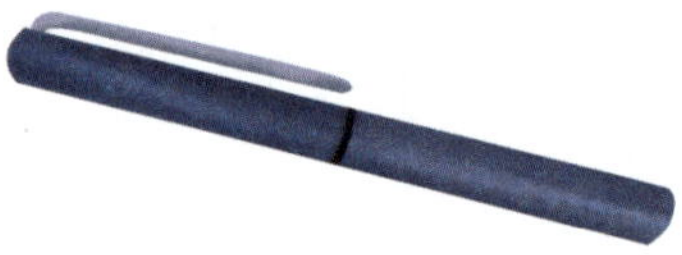

le **stylo**
[luh steeloh]

le **crayon**
[luh krayong]

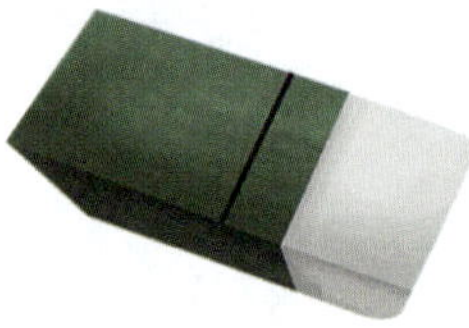

l'efface
[lefass]

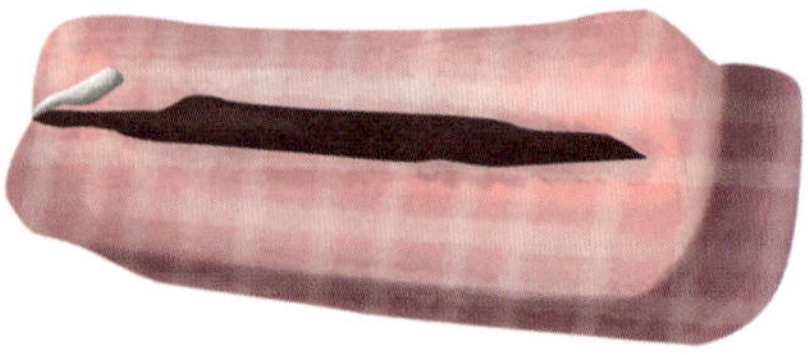

l'étui à crayons
[laytwee a krayong]

le **taille-crayon**
[luh tye-krayong]

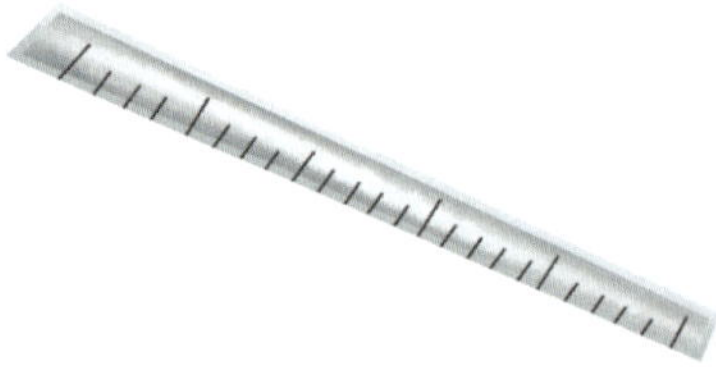

la **règle**
[la regl]

Playing "Kim's Game" is a great way to practise French vocabulary and can be used with the objects above. Place some of the above items on the table for others to see and remember (in French). When their eyes are closed, remove one object, saying **Qu'est-ce qu'il manque?** [kess keel mawnk] – **What's missing?** Of course, only answers in French will be accepted. This game can be used to practise colours (using pencil crayons) too.

Did you know? Quebec is the only province in Canada where school uniforms are worn in many schools.

Design your ideal pencil case. Remember to include a space for **les crayons**, **l'efface**, **les stylos** and anything else you want to keep in it. You might want to label it in French too.

Draw the correct number of items in each box. Practise counting as you draw.

huit (8) **crayons**

cinq (5) **effaces**

deux (2) **étuis à crayons**

Je sais...
I can...

On this page you can show how well you feel you have done while you have been learning French. Fill in the table to show your progress for each topic you have been learning.

très bien | bien | comme çi, comme ça

Je sais parler de... **I can talk about...**	
L'alphabet en français **The French alphabet**	
Moi **Me**	
Les nombres 1-10 **The numbers 1-10**	
Les nombres 11-20 **The numbers 11-20**	
Les couleurs **Colours**	
Ma famille **My family**	
Les animaux **Pets**	
Mon corps **My body**	
Mon visage **My face**	
Mon étui à crayons **My pencil case**	

Bravo! You have learned how to say so many things in French. Colour in the letters and pictures and fill in your name and date to make your very own personalized certificate.

Certificat de français

Très bien!

Certificat décerné à

____

pour avoir fait d'excellents progrès en français.

Date ____________________

La carte du Canada
Map of Canada

The map below shows where French is spoken as the main language in Canada.

Did you know? Quebec is the largest province in Canada. Nearly half of its population lives in Canada's second-biggest city, Montreal.

Did you know? Montreal is actually an island, and sits on the Saint Lawrence River. There are around 20 miles of tunnels underneath the city which people use every day to get from one place to another!

Did you know? The **Appalachian Mountains** stretch for 1500 miles from Newfoundland in Canada to Alabama in the United States.

La carte de l'Amérique du Nord

Map of North America

The map below shows North America and some of the countries that are nearby.

Additional suggestions for language practice

The next two pages give some suggestions for games and activities that can be used with larger groups of children, for example, in class or at French out-of-school organizations, holiday clubs, and so on.

It is often useful to have some basic commands in French and some of these listed below may be helpful. Most of the instructions are in the plural form to talk to more than one child.

Regardez-moi! [regarday mwa] meaning **Look at me!**

Levez la main! [luhvay la mang] meaning **Put up your hand!**

Levez-vous! [luhvay voo] meaning **Stand up!**

Dessinez…! [desseenay] meaning **Draw…!**

Allez-y! [allayzee] meaning **Get started!**

Écoutez! [aycootay] meaning **Listen!**

Arrêtez-vous! [arretay voo] meaning **Stop!**

Asseyez-vous! [assayay voo] meaning **Sit down!**

Écrivez votre nom! [aycreevay votr nom] meaning **Write your name!**

Allez! [allay] meaning **Go!**

Vite! [veet] meaning **Quickly!**

Doucement! [doosamong] meaning **Quietly!**

Lentement! [lawntamong] meaning **Slowly!**

Fort! [for] meaning **Loudly!**

Très bien! [treh beeyan] meaning **Very good!**

Bravo! [bravoe] meaning **Well done!**

Fantastique! [fantasteek] meaning **Fantastic!**

Gagné! [ganee-ay] meaning **You've won!**

Outdoor activities

Lots of activities can be played outside, including standard children's games but with a French twist. Here are just a few ideas:

- Send children off on a "Scavenger Hunt", looking for **quelque chose de vert/jaune/brun** and so on.
- Write numbers on the ground with chalk, shout out numbers or sums and children have to run to the correct one – this could also be played in teams.
- Children stand up against the wall and each is given one of 4 French words, for example, colours, pets, numbers and so on. One person stands in the middle and shouts out one of the words. The children who have been given that word try to run past the catcher in the middle without getting caught. Anyone caught helps to catch the others when they are called. Another version of this is where children stand in a circle and are each given one of 4 French words. One of the words is called out and the children who have been given that word have to run round the outside of the circle and back to their space. The last person back sits down.
- Use a parachute to practise colours – children have to run under the parachute to swap places with someone else who is also holding the colour that has been called out.

Did you know? Franco-Canadian children use this choosing rhyme (equivalent to **eeny, meeny, miny, mo**):
Un, deux, trois, quatre, Ma petite vache a mal aux pattes, Tirons-la par la queue,
Elle ira bien mieux, Dans un jour ou deux!

Active games

There are many ways to incorporate French into games which can be played in an indoor (or outdoor) space. Some examples of these are:

- Play "Corners" – put a picture in each corner of the area. The pictures could be of, for example, **les couleurs**, **la famille**, **les animaux**. Children move around the room and on a signal they go to stand in one of the corners. A corner is called out in French by the leader and the children in that corner are out. Keep playing until only a winner is left.
- Stand in a circle with the first child counting either 1 or 1, 2 or 1, 2, 3 in French and the next child continuing from there, saying an additional one, two or three numbers. Keep counting around the circle until someone says 13. That person then sits down and the game begins again, until there is only one person left.
- Ask children to move around the room – **vite/lentement** – and when they hear a part of the body they have to find a partner and touch those parts of the body together.
- Sit in a circle and give each child one of 4 or 5 French words belonging to a particular category, for example, pets, colours, family members. One child stands in the middle of the circle and calls out one of these words. Each child who has been given that word has to swap places with someone else with that word. The one person left in the middle is the next person to choose the word.

Quiet activities

There are lots of ideas to consolidate learning in French through activities that do not require too much space or moving around. Below are just a few ideas:

- Use building blocks to practise French numbers and colours – one child could describe a tower they have built and see if others can copy it without seeing it.
- "Consequences" is a fun way of reinforcing basic language. Each child has a piece of paper. At the top they have to answer the question **Comment tu t'appelles?** in a sentence, then fold over the paper and pass it to the person beside them. The next person answers the question **Tu as un animal?**, folds over the paper and passes it on. This can continue with questions and answers, with the paper being folded over and passed on each time. Finally, the paper is unfolded and the answers are read out – this game usually leads to some funny stories!
- Call out the alphabet, a letter at a time. If a child hears one of the letters in their name, they need to stand up and say **moi!** before sitting down again and waiting for the next letter.
- Dice are great for practising numbers and can also be used in other activities. Draw 6 pets and number them 1-6: ask a child to roll the dice and tell you which animal they have rolled. This could be used for other word categories, or extend the game from 1-12 and use two dice added together.

Traditional French games

Children often find it interesting to play games from another country and culture. Here are a few games which are played by Franco-Canadian children:

- **Un, deux, trois, soleil** - One person stands facing a wall while the others line up at the other end of the playground. The person with their back to the others calls **'un, deux, trois...'** while the others creep up on them. When the person shouts **'soleil'** and turns around, all the others have to be as still as statues. If they are seen moving they have to go back to the beginning. The winner is the one who makes it to the wall without being seen moving.
- **La marelle** - "Hopscotch" – draw out the hopscotch grid and use it to practise counting in French.
- **Roche, papier, ciseaux** – the classic game of "rock, paper, scissors".